I0087975

Abolitionist
Founding Fathers

Sin, Slavery and Redemption at America's Founding

Eddie L. Hyatt

HYATT PRESS

2021

America's Abolitionist Founding Fathers

By Eddie L. Hyatt
© 2021 by Hyatt International Ministries, Incorporated
ALL RIGHTS RESERVED.
Published by Hyatt Press
A Subsidiary of Hyatt Int'l Ministries, Incorporated

Mailing Address (2021)
Hyatt Int'l Ministries
P.O. Box 3877
Grapevine, TX 76099-3877

Internet Addresses
Email: dreddiehyatt@gmail.com
Web Site: www.eddiehyatt.com
Facebook: Eddie L. Hyatt

Unless otherwise indicated, all Scripture quotations are taken from the New King James Version of the Bible.

ISBN: 978-1-888435-64-1
Printed in the United States of America

Table of Contents

Preface

America's Founders are under attack. Their monuments are being toppled and their names removed from schools and other public buildings. School children are being taught that George Washington, Benjamin Franklin, and Thomas Jefferson were evil, rich slaveowners who founded this nation to protect their wealth and maintain the institution of slavery.

This "twisted history" is part of a larger plan to transform America into a Marxist/socialist society. George Orwell said, "Whoever controls the past, controls the future," and these socialists are well aware that their future plans for America have no hope unless they can "reframe" her past.

Enter the New York Times' "1619 Project" whose stated goal is just that—to "reframe" America's history. According to the 1619 narrative, America's true founding was 1619, when the first African slaves were brought to this land, not 1776. According to this narrative, America was forever defined by slavery and is racist and corrupt at her core and in need of radical transformation.

The 1619 narrative, of course, is not true. It is a twisted and distorted narrative driven by a political/ideological agenda. It highlights the bad and the ugly with no recognition of redemptive grace also at work in our nation's history.

Yes, slavery in America was real and is a blight on her history. But as one who believes in God's redemptive grace, this author clearly sees God's plan also at work in America's history. Take, for example, the Great Awakening that began in 1726 and the abolition movement that flowed out of it. All of Colonial America, including America's Founders, were impacted by this Awakening and the anti-slavery sentiments it unleashed.

This book does not ignore the sin of slavery in America's past but highlights God's redemptive grace at work in the midst of the sin. Indeed, as Roman 5:20 says, *But where sin abounded, grace did much more abound*.

When the whole story is heard, and the Founders are judged within the context of their own times, they emerge as revolutionaries at the forefront of the fight to put an end to slavery in the world. When the full truth is known, every American can be proud of their country's history and can sing together the words of that patriotic hymn,

> America! America! God shed His grace on thee,
> And crown thy good with brotherhood,
> From sea to shining sea.

Chapter I

Sin and Slavery

> *Slavery was, by no means, peculiar,*
> *odd, unusual, or unique to the U.S.*
> Dr. Walter Williams

Slavery has been practiced by many peoples and civilizations for thousands of years. Egyptians, Babylonians, Assyrians, Hittites, Greeks, Persians, Armenians, Arabs, and many others have practiced slavery. In describing the practice of slavery in the ancient Mediterranean world, the noted historian, Philip Schaff, said,

> The purchase and sale of slaves for from ten to seventy pieces of gold, according to their age, strength, and training, was a daily occurrence. All captives in war became slaves. The victory of Stilicho over Rhadagaisus (A.D. 406) threw 200,000 Goths and other Germans into the market and lowered the price of a slave from twenty-five pieces of gold to one. The capture and sale of men was part of the piratical system along all the shores of Europe.[1]

---

[1] Philip Schaff, vol. 3 *History of the Christian Church* (Grand Rapids: Eerdmans, 1994), 115-16.

The word "slavery" comes from the word "Slav" because so many ethnic Slavs were enslaved during the Middle Ages, and in more modern times millions were enslaved by the Turkish Ottoman Empire from 1300-1900. Decades after the Emancipation Proclamation in America, white slaves were still being bought and sold in the Islamic Ottoman Empire.

Throughout recorded history, people of all races and skin color have been enslaved and have enslaved others. Europeans enslaved Africans. Arabs enslaved both Africans and Europeans. Africans enslaved one another and sold their own people into slavery. African chiefs and businessmen greatly profited, along with Arabs and Europeans, by participating in the trans-Atlantic slave trade.

Native American tribes practiced slavery and when African slaves were brought to America, several native tribes enslaved black Africans. Descendants of those enslaved by the Cherokee, known as "freedmen," are now fighting for acceptance into the Cherokee tribe in Oklahoma.

Slavery and Sin Are Companions

Slavery is a horrible violation of human life and liberty. It came into the world at the time of the Fall (Genesis 3) when our first parents rebelled against their Creator and set out to build a human society apart from His guidance.

Only the Biblical account of the Fall makes sense of the presence of evil in the world. Only the Biblical account of sin explains how the same human species that built the pyramids, put a man on the moon, and has done so many good and noble deeds, also has a history filled with war, murder, lies, broken treaties, cruelty, hatred . . . and slavery.

Slavery in America
Neither Strange Nor Peculiar

Slavery being such a pervasive part of human history is why the late Dr. Walter E. Williams, Professor of Economics at George Mason University, said that slavery was, "by no means peculiar, odd, unusual, or unique to the U.S." He pointed out that at the beginning of the 19th century,

> An estimated three-quarters of all people alive were trapped in bondage against their will either in some form of slavery or serfdom.[2]

Williams said that what was strange and unique about slavery in America was the "moral outrage" that arose against it. The late historians, Elizabeth Fox-Genovese and Eugene Genovese, agreed, saying,

> Europeans [and Americans] did not outdo others in enslaving people or treating slaves viciously. They

---

[2] Walter Williams, "Slavery is Neither Strange Nor Peculiar," *The Daily Home*, May 28; https://tinyurl.com/zs73k2

8

outdid others by creating a Christian civilization that eventually stirred moral condemnation of slavery and roused mass movements against it.

America's Founders Turned Against Slavery

The brilliant economist and historian, Dr. Thomas Sowell, has made the same point. He notes that although slavery has been a world-wide phenomenon, practiced by peoples and civilizations for thousands of years, it only became controversial in the 18th century in Western civilization and particularly in America. He says,

Slavery was just not an issue, not even among intellectuals, much less among political leaders, until the 18th century— and then it was an issue only in Western civilization. Among those who turned against slavery in the 18th century were George Washington, Thomas Jefferson, Patrick Henry, and other American leaders. You could research all of 18th century Africa or Asia or the Middle East without finding any comparable rejection of slavery there.[3]

Concerning the time frame of this modern anti-slavery movement, the Genoveses came to the same conclusion as Sowell and wrote,

---

[3] Thomas Sowell, "Twisted History," https://townhall.com/columnists/thomassowell/2003/12/17/twisted-history-n1057496

Perception of slavery as morally unacceptable — as sinful — did not become widespread until the second half of the eighteenth century.

The Source of the Moral Outrage

This raises the question as to the source of this 18th century "moral outrage" that arose against slavery in the Western world, and particularly in America? The answer is found in a great, spiritual awakening that ebbed and flowed in Colonial America from 1726 to 1770.

In this Christian awakening, entire towns turned to God and were morally transformed. Racial and cultural barriers were breached and an abolition movement arose that impacted all of America, including America's Founders.

Chapter 2

Racial Barriers Breached In a Great Awakening

> *It was under the impulse of the revival that the chasm between white and black cultures was breached.*
> Dr. Mark Noll

A great, spiritual awakening, beginning in 1726, morally transformed Colonial America. This Christian revival breached racial and cultural barriers, ignited an abolition movement, and paved the way for the formation of the United States of America.

This Christian revival began among the Dutch Reformed of New Jersey when a young Dutch Reformed pastor, Theodore Frelinghuysen, began visiting his flock in their homes and pointing out, both in person and from the pulpit, their un-Christian behavior and their spiritual apathy.

Many were morally transformed and testified of a "new birth" experience. Churches overflowed and the revival spread to other Dutch Reformed churches and then to the Presbyterian churches in the region.

A young Presbyterian pastor, Gilbert Tennant, was awakened and began to preach that many had placed their faith on unreliable foundations such as church membership, family pedigree, and good works. He called people to repentance and to an unfettered faith in Jesus Christ. Many Presbyterians testified to being "born again" as the revival spread throughout the Middle Colonies touching those of every sect and denomination.

Revival in New England

As revival was spreading throughout the Middle Colonies, it also began to break forth in New England among the descendants of the Puritans. Jonathan Edwards (1703-1758), pastor of the Congregational Church in Northampton, Massachusetts, had been concerned by what he described as "the general deadness throughout the land," and he and his wife, Sarah, had set themselves to seek God for a "revival of religion."[4]

As Jonathan, Sarah, and others prayed, an unusual sense of God's presence seemed to fill the entire community of Northampton during the spring and summer of 1735. Edwards reported, "The town seemed to be full of the presence of God." In every part of town, the Spirit of God was powerfully at work until "there was scarcely a single person in the town, old or young, left unconcerned about the great things of the eternal world."[5]

---

[4] David S. Lovejoy, *Religious Enthusiasm and the Great Awakening* (Englewood Cliffs, NJ: Prentice Hall, 1969), 5.

[5] Jonathan Edwards, *Jonathan Edwards on Revival* (Carlisle, PA: Banner of Truth Trust, 1994), 13.

Without any sort of planned evangelistic outreach, "souls did as it were come by flocks to Jesus Christ."[6] Instead of resorting to the tavern, people now crowded Edwards' home clamoring to hear the message of Christ and His salvation. His home, Edwards said, "was thronged far more than ever the tavern had been wont to be."[7] He went on to say,

> Our public assemblies were then beautiful: the congregation was alive in God's service, everyone intent on the public worship, every hearer eager to drink in the words of the minister as they came from his mouth; the assembly were in general from time to time in tears while the word was preached; some weeping with sorrow and distress, others with joy and love, others with pity and concern for the souls of their neighbors.[8]

George Whitefield

The young Methodist evangelist, George Whitefield, arrived in America on his first of seven visits in 1738. He travelled up and down the eastern seaboard and everywhere he preached, farmers left their plows, mechanics threw down their tools, and women left their chores to go to the place where he was to preach.

Crowds of 10,000 and more were common, and it is estimated that 20,000 gathered on the Boston Common to

---

[6] Edwards, 13.

[7] Edwards, 24.

[8] Edwards, 14.

hear Whitefield preach when the population of Boston was only 17,000. Through his incessant travels, Whitefield was able to spread the fires of the many regional revivals into one blazing inferno of Divine awakening. This is what historians have called the "Great Awakening."

In his *Autobiography*, Benjamin Franklin described the amazing transformation of his hometown of Philadelphia when Whitefield preached there in 1739 to massive crowds from the steps of the courthouse. He wrote,

> It was wonderful to see the change soon made in the manners of our inhabitants. The multitudes of all sects and denominations that attended his sermons were enormous, and it was a matter of speculation to me, who was one of the number, to observe the extraordinary influence of his oratory on his hearers. From being thoughtless or indifferent about religion, it seemed as if all the world were growing religious so that one could not walk through the town in an evening without hearing psalms sung in different families of every street.[9]

Racial Barriers Come Down

The preachers of the Great Awakening saw all people—regardless of social status, race, or gender—as being under the power and penalty of sin, with only one remedy: faith in Jesus Christ. In other words, whether a

---

[9] Benjamin Franklin, *The Autobiography of Benjamin Franklin* (New York City: Airmont Publ., 1965), 100.

person was of high or low standing in society, whether a person was rich or poor, whether male or female, and whether slave or free was all irrelevant when it came to forgiveness of sins through faith in Jesus Christ.

Moved by this theological understanding and stirred by the power of the Awakening, many reached across cultural divides to share the Good News with those who had been relegated to the margins of Colonial American society.

Women, Native Americans, and those of African descent all participated together in the Great Awakening.[10] Mark Noll, Professor of Church History at Wheaton College, has said, "It was under the impulse of the revival that the chasm between White and black cultures was breached."[11]

Whitefield's *Journals* confirm that blacks and whites freely worshipped together in the Awakening in Philadelphia. For example, after preaching his farewell message in Philadelphia and retiring to his lodging, hundreds came to wish him farewell.

Among the well-wishers were many blacks, for Whitefield recorded in his *Journal* that, "Near 50 Negroes came to give me thanks for what God had done for their souls." He considered this an answer to prayer, saying, "I

---

[10] See my book, *1726: The Year that Defined America*, for a more detailed account of the impact of the Awakening on women and Native Americans.

[11] Mark Noll, *A History of Christianity in the United States and Canada* (Grand Rapids: Eerdmans, 1992), 107.

have been much drawn in prayer for them, and have seen them wrought upon by the word preached." [12]

Whitefield also tells of a black woman, who had been converted under his ministry in Philadelphia, becoming discouraged and praying that the Lord would manifest Himself to her. The answer to her prayer came on a particular day when a Baptist minister was preaching.

Whitefield was in the meeting and said that the word came with such power that the woman began to cry out and "could not help praising and blessing God." When some criticized her for interrupting the preacher, Whitefield came to her defense saying he believed that in that hour, "the Lord Jesus took a great possession of her soul." [13]

He went on to say, "I doubt not, when the poor Negroes are to be called, God will highly favor them, to wipe off their reproach, and show that He is no respecter of persons." [14]

A Black Poet Honors Whitefield

Whitefield's impact among the black populace of Colonial America was highlighted by the moving tribute that a young black woman, Phillis Wheatley, who later became America's first published black poet, wrote in his honor at the time of his death.

---

[12] http://www.chitorch.org/index.php/chm/seventeenth-century/slave-religion/2/

[13] Whitefield, 420.

[14] Whitefield, 420.

Wheatley had been sold into slavery by an African chief at the age of seven. She was purchased by the Wheatley family of Boston who treated her like a daughter and encouraged her in her poetic gift.

She, no doubt, heard Whitefield preach during his numerous visits to Boston and may have been converted under his ministry. The words of her poem express the inclusive strains that were heard in the Gospel he preached. It reads in part,

> *Thou didst in strains of eloquence refined,*
> *Inflame the heart and captivate the mind.*
> *The greatest gift that even God can give,*
> *He freely offered to the numerous throng.*
> *Take him, ye Africans, he longs for you,*
> *Impartial Savior is his title due.*

Wheatley obviously quoted directly from Whitefield's preaching in her poem. Knowing Whitefield's passionate form of preaching, one can picture him crying out to blacks in his audience, "Take him, ye Africans, he longs for you."

This must have been the case in Philadelphia where many blacks were left weeping and in awe after Whitfield's message. One black woman, after hearing Whitefield preach, stated that he must have been in a trance and insisted that "Jesus Christ must have told him what to speak to the people or else he could not speak as he did."[15]

---

[15] Thomas S. Kidd, *George Whitefield:* America's *Spiritual Founding*

Other Outreaches to Africans

Whitefield was not alone in his desire to reach the American black population with the Gospel. Further south, Samuel Davies, a Presbyterian minister who served as president of the College of New Jersey (now Princeton University), gave special attention to blacks, including slaves, during his time of ministry in Virginia. He was greatly encouraged by their enthusiastic response to the Gospel and wrote,

> My principal encouragement of late has been among the poor negro slaves; in the land of their slavery they have been brought into the glorious liberty of the sons of God.

Davies not only preached to blacks, both slave and free, he treated them as brothers and sisters in Christ, inviting them to share in regular church observances including the Lord's Supper. In 1757 he wrote,

> What little success I have lately had, has been chiefly among the extremes of Gentlemen and Negroes. Indeed, God has been remarkably working among the latter. I have baptized 150 adults; and at the last sacramental solemnity, I had the pleasure of seeing the table graced with sixty black faces.[16]

Father (New Haven: Yale University Press, 2014), 114.

[16] Mark Noll, *A History of Christianity in the United States and Canada* (Grand Rapids: Eerdmans, 1996), 106-07.

Back to the north, Gilbert Tennent was delighted that during a preaching tour in Massachusetts, "multitudes were awakened, and several received great consolation, especially among the young people, children, and Negroes." Edwards, in his account of the Awakening in his hometown of Northampton, mentions "several Negroes" who appeared to have been truly born again.

Positive Fruit of the Awakening

The Awakening led to the humanizing of slaves and a general awakening to the evils of the institution of slavery. It also led to the emergence of new, black congregations, among those who were enslaved and those who were free. This then led to many blacks identifying with the struggle for freedom from Great Britain and becoming part of the patriotic protests, especially in New England.

At the time of the Boston Massacre in April of 1770, a black man, Crispus Attucks, was one of the leaders in the protests against the occupation of Boston by British troops. An escaped slave who had settled in Boston, he was one of those of those killed that day by British soldiers. A poem written in his honor referred to him as,

Leader and voice that day;
the first to defy and the first to die.[17]

---

[17] T. Harry Williams, Richard N. Current, and Frank Freidel, *A History of the United States to 1877* (New York: Random House, 1959), 132.

The positive ripples from the Awakening also opened the way for blacks to later serve in the Revolutionary Army. General George Washington, in fact, instructed his recruiters to welcome free blacks into the ranks of the American army. As a result, one in every seven soldiers was of African descent.

blacks and Whites thus fought together for freedom from Great Britain. David Barton has provided documentation showing that numbers of blacks were given honorable discharges and pensions, and some were honored with complete military funerals for their service in the War.[18]

The Awakening also released currents of anti-slavery sentiments. The opposition to slavery was so strong in the North that when separation with Great Britain came in 1776, immediately, several states, including Pennsylvania, Massachusetts, Connecticut, Rhode Island, Vermont, New Hampshire, and New York took steps to abolish slavery, something they could not do under King George III.

Although there was more resistance in the South, where a monetary motive prevailed, the anti-slavery sentiments released by the Awakening flowered into an abolition movement that would impact the entire populace of Colonial America, including America's Founders.

---

[18] David Barton, "Glen Beck," The Fox News Channel, May 27, 2011.

Chapter 3

Abolition Begins

> *Slavery is a work of the flesh, assisted by the devil; a mystery of iniquity, that works like witchcraft to darken your understanding, and harden your hearts against conviction.*
>
> James O'Kelly, Methodist Revivalist

At the beginning of the Awakening in 1726, outreach to the black populace was evangelistic in nature and not characterized by opposition to slavery. Those early preachers, such as Whitefield, Tennant, Edwards, and others, saw their primary purpose to be in getting people ready for the next world, not necessarily improving their lot in this one. In their thinking, a slave on his way to heaven was far better off than a king on his way to hell.

Nonetheless, their compassion for Blacks, both slave and free, and their willingness to share Christian fellowship with them broke down racial and cultural barriers. Their preaching and actions created a climate conducive to the anti-slavery sentiments that would burst forth through the preaching of those who came after them.

The Attack on Slavery Begins

Evangelists who came after Edwards, Tennant, and Whitefield carried the message of their predecessors to its logical conclusion: if we are all creatures of the same Creator and if Christ died that all might be saved, then how can slavery ever be justified?

They began, therefore, not only to offer salvation to individuals, but to viciously attack the institution of slavery as sinful and evil in the sight of God. This is what historian, Benjamin Hart, was referring to when he wrote, "Among the most ardent opponents of slavery were ministers, particularly the Puritan and revivalist preachers."[19]

These "ardent opponents of slavery" included the followers of Jonathan Edwards who expanded on his idea of the essential dignity of all created beings and applied it to the Blacks of Colonial America.

Samuel Hopkins (1721–1803), for example, who had been personally tutored by Edwards, pastored for a time in Newport, Rhode Island, an important hub in the transatlantic slave trade. Like Paul, whose spirit was "provoked" observing the idols in Athens, Hopkins was outraged by the "violation of God's will" he observed in Newport and declared, "This whole country have their hands full of blood this day."[20]

---

[19] Benjamin Hart, *Faith & Freedom*: Dallas: Lewis and Stanley, 1988), 330.

[20] Thomas S. Kidd, *God of Liberty* (New York: Basic Books, 2010), 153.

After the First Continental Congress convened in Philadelphia in 1774, Hopkins sent a pamphlet to every member of the Congress, asking how they could complain about "enslavement" to Great Britain and overlook the "enslavement" of so many Blacks in the colonies.

Indeed, as "liberty" became a watchword throughout the colonies, the preachers of the Awakening began applying it to the enslaved Blacks in America. Like Hopkins, they pointed out the hypocrisy of demanding freedom from Great Britain while enslaving Black Africans.

The influence of these ministers spread to others in church, business, and government. For example, James Otis, Jr., a lawyer and member of the Massachusetts provincial assembly, called slavery "the most shocking violation of the law of nature" and a vice "that makes every dealer in it a petty tyrant."[21]

In a sermon preached and published in 1770, Samuel Cooke declared that by tolerating the evil of slavery, "We, the patrons of liberty, have dishonored the Christian name, and degraded human nature nearly to a level with the beasts that perish."[22]

The Baptist preacher, John Allen, was even more direct, and thundered,

---

[21] Hart, 330.

[22] "How the American Revolution Shed Light on the Moral Problem of Slavery," *The Founding*, https://thefounding.net/the-american-revolution-shed-light-on-and-helped-to-abolish-slavery/; quoted in Hart, 330.

23

Blush ye pretended votaries of freedom! ye trifling Patriots! who are making a vain parade of being advocates for the liberties of mankind, who are thus making a mockery of your profession by trampling on the sacred natural rights and privileges of Africans.[23]

The Opposition Expands

The opposition continued to grow and the anonymous author of the popular, *A Discourse on the Times*, declared that if Americans would have the Lord on their side, "We must set at liberty those vast number of Africans, which have so long time been enslaved by us, who have as good a right to liberty as we have."[24]

David Avery, the chaplain who prayed over the minutemen at Bunker Hill (1775), declared that if the states would begin the process of emancipating the slaves, it would be "a pleasing omen of the happy issue of our present struggle for liberty."[25]

Freeborn Garrettson Hears God

Freeborn Garrettson (1752-1827), an evangelist from Maryland, freed his slaves after hearing God speak to him supernaturally. According to Garrettson, he heard the Lord say, "It is not right for you to keep your fellow

---

[23] John Coffey, *Exodus and Liberation* (Oxford: Oxford Univ. Press, 2014), 91; quoted in Hart, 330.

[24] *A Discourse on the Times* (Norwich, CT, 1776); quoted in Kidd, *God of Liberty*, 154.

[25] Kidd, *God of Liberty*, 154

creatures in bondage; you must let the oppressed go free."

Garrettson immediately informed his slaves that they did not belong to him and that he did not desire their services without giving them proper compensation.

Garrettson began preaching against slavery and advocating for freedom, which provoked intense opposition, especially in the South. One enraged slave-owner came to the house where Garrettson was lodging and swore at him, threatened him, and punched him in the face. Garrettson did not retaliate but sought to reason with the man who finally gave up and left.

Garrettson took his message to North Carolina where he preached to Black audiences and sought to "inculcate the doctrine of freedom in them."[26] His opposition to slavery was firmly rooted in the Gospel and he described a typical meeting with slaves in which,

> Many of their sable faces were bedewed with tears, their withered hands of faith were stretched out, and their precious souls made white in the blood of the Lamb.[27]

Garrettson also preached to southern White audiences and sought to convince them of the sinfulness and evil character of slavery and that God's will was liberty for all His creatures.

---

[26] Freeborn Garretson, *The Experience and Travels of Mr. Freeborn Garretson* (Philadelphia, 1791); quoted in Kidd, *God of Liberty*, 160.

[27] Garretson, *The Experience and Travels of Mr. Freeborn Garretson*; quoted in Kidd, *God of Liberty*, 160.

In Delaware, Garrettson visited the Stokeley Sturgis plantation and preached to both the slaves and the Sturgis family. He was able to convince Sturgis that slavery is a sin and Sturgis began making arrangements for his slaves to obtain freedom.

Richard Allen, Methodist Revivalist

One slave, Richard Allen, obtained his freedom and became a successful Methodist evangelist to both Black and White audiences. In 1784, he preached for weeks in Radnor, Pennsylvania to mostly White audiences and recalled hearing them say, "This man must be a man of God; I have never heard such preaching before."[28]

Allen became close friends with one of America's Founding Fathers, Benjamin Rush, a Philadelphia physician, member of the Continental Congress, and a signer of the Declaration of Independence. As the Awakening waned, the Methodist Church in Philadelphia, of which Allen was a member, decided to segregate congregational seating according to race. Allen and other Blacks walked out.

Rush, a Presbyterian, came to their aid with both moral and financial support. He assisted them in obtaining property and erecting their own building in which to

---

[28] Richard Allen, *The Life, Experiences, and Gospel Labours of the Right Rev. Richard Allen* (Philadelphia, 1833), 5-8, 10, 16; quoted in Kidd, *God of Liberty*, 197.

worship. They established Bethel Methodist Church out which came the African Methodist Episcopal (AME) denomination. Allen later wrote,

> We had waited on Dr. Rush and Mr. Robert Ralston, and told them of our distressing situation. We considered it a blessing that the Lord had put it into our hearts to wait upon those gentlemen. They pitied our situation, and subscribed largely towards the church, and were very friendly towards us and advised us how to go on . . . Dr. Rush did much for us in public by his influence. I hope the name of Dr. Benjamin Rush and Mr. Robert Ralston will never be forgotten among us. They were the two first gentlemen who espoused the cause of the oppressed and aided us in building the house of the Lord for the poor Africans to worship in. Here was the beginning and rise of the first African church in America.[29]

Think about it! One of America's Founding Fathers played an important role in the founding of one of the largest and most respected Black denominations in America.

It was out of the Great Awakening that the American Black church was born and became a positive force in American society, producing some of the nation's greatest

---

[29] https://en.wikipedia.org/wiki/Benjamin_Rush.

preachers, singers, and musicians. Indeed, the Civil Rights movement of the 1960s-70s was anchored in the Black churches of America and its most prominent leaders, such as Dr. Martin Luther King, Jr., (1929-1968) were ordained ministers—a legacy of the Great Awakening.

The Methodists

In 1744, John Wesley (1703–1791) spoke publicly against slavery, declaring that, in God's sight, Blacks are equal with Whites and that Christ died for all. Many Methodists in America, in both the North and South, picked up on Wesley's call and became some of the leading abolitionists in America.

James O'Kelly (1735-1826), for example, faced physical attacks because of his bold, excoriating preaching against slavery. He painted slaveholding as a debilitating and demonic kind of sin. It was, he said,

> A work of the flesh, assisted by the devil; a mystery of iniquity, that works like witchcraft to darken your understanding, and harden your hearts against conviction.[30]

Because of the bold preaching of Garrettson, O'Kelly, and many others, there emerged an anti-slavery movement, even in in the South. This movement faced intense opposition, as was the case in 1800 when South Carolina Methodists circulated a petition calling for emancipation.

---

[30] Kidd, *God of Liberty*, 160.

A mob burned the handouts and dragged one of the Methodist preachers through the streets and almost drowned him in a well.

Nonetheless, the anti-slavery sentiments continued to grow. In fact, the movement so permeated Methodism that a 1784 gathering of Methodist leaders in Baltimore denounced slavery as "contrary to the golden rule of God . . . and the unalienable rights of mankind, as well as every principle of the Revolution."[31]

They went a step further, requiring all members of Methodist churches, including in the South, to begin emancipating their slaves. Those who refused to do so were to be expelled from the church.

However, six months later, the demand was withdrawn because of the backlash in the South and due to allegations that the anti-slavery proponents were, in fact, British agents seeking to stir up a race war. Nonetheless, from this point forward, the South was on the defensive about the issue of slavery.

Many supporters of the practice scrambled to devise moral arguments to justify the institution. A commonly proposed argument was that it was God's way of bringing Africans from their pagan land to expose them to the Gospel.

Samuel Hopkins, however, dismantled this argument in his pamphlet entitled, *A Dialogue Concerning the Slavery of*

---

[31] Kidd, *God of Liberty*, 159,

Africans: Shewing It To Be the Duty and Interest of the American Colonies to Emancipate All the African Slaves. Although Hopkins would acknowledge God's providence working out his plan even through human acts of sin (as in the Old Testament story of Joseph), he condemned this argument as merely an excuse for slavery. He thundered,

> What sort of "gospel" message is being conveyed when people are enslaved because of the color of their skin? The Declaration of Independence says all men are created equal with certain unalienable rights. Oh, the shocking, the intolerable inconsistencies![32]

The Quakers

The Society of Friends, commonly known as Quakers, became some of the most ardent opponents of slavery in the New World. This is not surprising since one of their cardinal beliefs was the equality of all people before God. They rejected the idea of hierarchy in both the church and society.

From their beginnings in England in the latter half of the 1600s, they lived this out in various ways. For example, they refused to show the expected honor to the upper classes by doffing their hats and by addressing them by their titles. This resulted in many of them being whipped

---

[32] *A Dialogue Concerning the Slavery of Africans: Shewing It To Be the Duty and Interest of the American Colonies to Emancipate All the African Slaves,* https://digitalcollections.nypl.org/items/510d47e3-f853-a3d9-e040-e00a18064a99#/?uuid=510d47e3-f889-a3d9-e040-e00a18064a99.

and imprisoned, where hundreds died due to the filthy prison conditions.

It is, therefore, not surprising that when George Fox (1624-1691), the founder of Quakerism, visited the English colony of Barbados in 1671, he appealed to the Quakers there to consider freeing their slaves. They should do this, he said, because not only are they equal by virtue of creation, but also because Christ died for all races.[33]

After Fox's visit, Quaker colonists in Barbados began questioning slavery and then denounced it openly in 1688. That same year, a joint meeting of Lutherans and Quakers in Germantown, Pennsylvania, issued a protest concerning the existence of slavery in the newly formed colony of Philadelphia.

In her excellent article entitled "The Good Fruit Remains," Dr. Susan Hyatt says,

> In 1657, Fox had written a letter denouncing the captivity of Black and Indian slaves. The Friends [Quakers] were actually the first to make a direct assault against slavery. Sixty years before the Emancipation Proclamation (January 1, 1863), there was not one Quaker slaveholder in America. In the mid-nineteenth century, they conducted the underground railroad providing for the safe passage of escaped and freed slaves to the Canadian border.[34]

---

[33] Kidd, God of Liberty, 134.

[34] Susan Hyatt, "The Good Fruit Remains," http://www.icwhp.org/quakers.html.

Compelling Moral Arguments

The moral arguments against slavery were both obvious and compelling. These arguments were rooted in both Creation and Redemption. Creation tells us that all people are equal for the genealogy of all humanity begins with Adam and Eve. There is also equality in Redemption, for Christ died for all and His salvation is equally available to all who will believe. The old value systems that judged a person on the basis of race, sex, and class were abolished in Christ (Galatians 3:27-28).

The Golden Rule was also used as an argument against slavery. David Barrow (1753–1819), a Baptist preacher from Virginia who freed his slaves and became an abolitionist, simply referred to "having a single eye to the Golden Rule" as the basis for emancipation. He insisted that if everyone practiced "Do to all men as you would they should do to you," it would soon put an end to slavery.

A Stunning Resolution

The impact of the Great Awakening, and the anti-slavery sentiments it spawned, are obvious on the Founders from the very beginning of the nation. When the First Continental Congress met at Carpenter's Hall in Philadelphia for the first time on September 5, 1774, they opened with an extended time of Bible reading and prayer.

Representatives from all 13 colonies, except Georgia, had met to consider a response to the oppressive, Intolerable Acts that had been imposed upon them by the British. They were also deeply concerned that British soldiers, who had been sent to enforce these Intolerable Acts, had occupied the city of Boston and closed its port.

Among the numerous resolutions passed by this Congress, was a resolution stating that the slave trade should be abolished and that nations engaged in it should be boycotted.

Historian, Christian M. McBurney, called this ban on the slave trade "a stunning and radical move" and "the first nationally organized antislavery effort in American history, and one of the first in world history.[35]

After pushback from southern delegates, the ban was later modified, leaving it to the individual states to decide. Nonetheless, by the time of the Constitutional Convention 13 years later, every state except Georgia had banned or suspended the importation of slaves into the United States.

This is a vivid example how the Awakening, and the abolition movement it had spawned, was influencing Colonial America and the Founders even at this early and strategic time.

---

[35] Christian M. McBurney, "The First Efforts to Limit the African Slave Trade Arise in the American Revolution: Part 3 of 3, Congress Bans the African Slave Trade," *Journal of the American Revolution*, https://tinyurl.com/hesrnbu6.

Chapter 4

America's Founders
Turn Against Slavery

> *Among those who turned against slavery in the 18th century were George Washington, Thomas Jefferson, Patrick Henry, and other American leaders. You could research all of 18th century Africa or Asia or the Middle East without finding any comparable rejection of slavery there.*
>
> Thomas Sowell

By the time of the writing of the Declaration of Independence in 1776 and the Constitution in 1787, virtually every Founder, even those who still owned slaves, had taken a public stand against slavery.

Thomas Jefferson, for example, called slavery a "moral depravity" and "hideous blot" and said it presented the greatest threat to the future survival of America. James Madison, America's 4th president, called slavery "the most oppressive dominion ever exercised by man over man."

Gouverneur Morris, Founding Father from Pennsylvania, gave a blazing anti-slavery speech at the Constitutional Convention. He called slavery a "nefarious practice" that stood "in defiance of the most sacred laws of humanity." Commenting on his speech, James Madison said that Morris viewed slavery with "a laudable horror."

This anti-slavery stance of the Founders was unique on the world stage, for as Sowell said, "You could research all of 18th century Africa or Asia or the Middle East without finding any comparable rejection of slavery there."

The following are 7 of America's most renowned Founders with their views on slavery.

John Adams

John Adams (1735-1826) was one of the most influential of the Founding Fathers. He served as the first Vice-President under George Washington and then as the nation's 2nd president after Washington retired.

A lawyer from Massachusetts, Adams was one of the most learned and influential men in Colonial America. The historian, William Novak, says, "No single man is more responsible for the Fourth of July, and the independence for which it stands, than John Adams."[36]

Adams never owned slaves and was throughout his life a passionate abolitionist who described slavery as a "foul contagion in the human character" and "an evil of colossal

---

[36] Novak, 147.

magnitude." He insisted,

> Every measure of prudence ought to be assumed for the eventual total extirpation of slavery from the United States . . . I have throughout my whole life held the practice of slavery in abhorrence. [37]

Benjamin Franklin

Benjamin Franklin (1706-1790) was one of the most respected of America's Founding Fathers. He was a member of the Continental Congress and served on a select committee of five given the task of assisting Thomas Jefferson in formulating the Declaration of Independence.

From 1776 to 1785 Franklin served as Ambassador to France for the newly formed United States of America. He achieved great success in that capacity, securing the assistance of the French in the war against Great Britain. He was also the chief American negotiator for peace with Great Britain that eventually led to the signing of the Treaty of Paris. The Treaty of Paris, which he signed on September 3, 1783, ended the Revolutionary War.

---

[37] From John Adams to Robert J. Evans, 8 June 1819, https://founders.archives.gov/documents/Adams/99-02-02-7148.

In 1785, Franklin freed his two slaves, who had served him as household servants, and began advocating for abolition. He joined the "Pennsylvania Society for Promoting the Abolition of Slavery" and later served as its president. In a public address to this society, Franklin called slavery, "an atrocious debasement of human nature" and "a source of serious evils."

Benjamin Rush

Dr. Benjamin Rush (1745-1813) was a Philadelphia physician, member of the Continental Congress, and signer of the Declaration of Independence. He also served as Professor of Chemistry and Medical Theory at the University of Pennsylvania and was appointed by Washington to be Surgeon General during the Revolutionary War.

Rush was a passionate abolitionist who helped form America's first Abolition society in his hometown of Philadelphia in 1774. As mentioned earlier, he assisted the former slave and Methodist evangelist, Richard Allen, in establishing Bethel Methodist Church in Philadelphia, out of which emerged the African Methodist Episcopal (AME) denomination.

A devout Christian, he called on the pastors and ministers of America to take a bold stand against slavery, which he called a "hydra sin." He wrote,

But chiefly—ye ministers of the gospel, whose

dominion over the principles and actions of men is so universally acknowledged and felt, - Ye who estimate the worth of your fellow creatures by their immortality, and therefore must look upon all mankind as equal; - let your zeal keep pace with your opportunities to put a stop to slavery. While you enforce the duties of "tithe and cumin," neglect not the weightier laws of justice and humanity. Slavery is a Hydra sin and includes in it every violation of the precepts of the Laws and the Gospels.[38]

Alexander Hamilton

Alexander Hamilton (1755-1804) served as chief of staff for General George Washington during the Revolutionary War and became the nation's first Secretary of the Treasury. A lawyer from New York, he also served in Congress and was a delegate to the Constitutional Convention in 1787. In defense of the new Constitution, he wrote 51 of the 85 installments of the *Federalist Papers*, which are still used as one of the most important references for interpreting the Constitution.

Hamilton was passionate about ending slavery and in 1785 he and others founded the "New York Society for Promoting

---

[38] Benjamin Rush, "On Slavekeeping" (1773), found in William Bennett, *Our Sacred Honor* (New York: Simon and Schuster, 1997), 376-77.

the Manumission of Slaves." Both "manumission" and "abolition" referred to the freeing of slaves. "Manumission," however, emphasized that slaveholders should take initiative and free their slaves even if there was not yet any law against it, simply because it was the right thing to do.

The Preamble to the founding document of this society, which Hamilton helped author, refers to slaves as "our Brethren" and states that it is their goal to enable them to "share equally" in the civil and religious liberties the nation had obtained from Great Britain. They wrote,

> The benevolent Creator and Father of Men, having given to them all an equal Right to Life, Liberty and Property, no Sovereign Power on Earth can justly deprive them of either. It is our Duty therefore, both as free Citizens and Christians, not only to regard with compassion the injustice done to those among us who are held as slaves, but endeavor, by lawful ways and means, to enable them to share equally with us in that civil and religious Liberty with which an indulgent Providence has blessed these States; and to which these, our Brethren are by nature, as much entitled as ourselves.

Hamilton became a counsellor-at-law for the society, charged with the duty of suggesting changes to state laws for ending slavery and defending in court freed slaves who had been taken captive or forced back into servitude.

One year before the Constitutional Convention, in March of 1786, he signed a petition to the New York legislature demanding the immediate abolishment of the slave trade, which he and the other signers called,

> A commerce so repugnant to humanity, and inconsistent with the liberality of justice, which should distinguish a free and enlightened people.[39]

In 1787, the society opened the doors of the African Free School in New York City. It was established to educate Black children and prepare them for success in the new nation.

Historian, Ron Chernow, praised Hamilton as an "unwavering abolitionist who saw emancipation of the slaves as an inseparable part of the struggle for freedom." He also lauded Hamilton for never owning slaves, which is in line with what Hamilton's son said of his father.

Some modern researchers think they have found evidence that Hamilton did own slaves. It is interesting, however, that neither Hamilton's son nor his earliest biographers knew of this. It makes one wonder if these researchers, like the creators of the "1619 Project," began their research with a predetermined conclusion and merely found what they were looking for.

What is clear and undeniable about Hamilton is that, like the other Founders, he turned against slavery in the 18th

---

[39] "Memorial to Abolish the Slave Trade," *Founders Online*, https://founders.archives.gov/documents/Hamilton/01-03-02-0503

century and worked hard to bring about its demise in America.

George Washington

George Washington (1732-1799) was the most respected person in 18th century America because of his leadership abilities, character, and selfless sacrifice in leading the Colonial Army to victory over the British. He is the only president to be elected with every electoral vote; and this happened, not once, but twice.

Although born in Virginia into a slave-owning family, Washington came to abhor slavery as did most other Founders. In a letter to Robert Morris, dated April 12, 1786, he said, "There is not a man living who wishes more sincerely than I do, to see a plan adopted for the abolition of slavery."

When, in 1775, the young Black poet, Phyllis Wheatley, sent Washington a poem written in his honor, he commended her and invited her to visit him at his army headquarters in Cambridge, MA. She did so the following year and had a cordial visit with General Washington who expressed his admiration for her and encouraged her to continue in her work.

Before his death, Washington devised a plan to completely rid Mt. Vernon of slavery. Those slaves who chose to leave were free to do so and those who chose to stay were paid wages. He also began a program to educate the children of slaves and prepare them for liberty. In a conversation with John Bernard concerning abolition, Washington declared,

> Not only do I pray for it, on the score of human dignity, but I can clearly foresee that nothing but the rooting out of slavery can perpetuate the existence of our union by consolidating it in a common bond of principle.[40]

Patrick Henry

Patrick Henry (1736-1799) is a Founding Father who served as a member of the Continental Congress and as governor of Virginia. He is best known for his passionate speech, "Give me Liberty of Give Me Death," in which he called for independence from Great Britain.

Henry is an example of those who lived with the contradiction of confessing that slavery was sinful and wrong, while continuing to own slaves out of long-held practice and personal convenience.

Henry, for example, spoke passionately against slavery in a letter to the Virginia Quaker, Robert Pleasants (1723–1801), who had sent Henry an anti-slavery tract, and informed him that he had freed his slaves.

---

[40] John Bernard, *Retrospections of America, 1797-1811*, 91; quoted by Hart, 332.

In his response, Henry expressed complete agreement with Pleasants, calling slavery a "lamentable evil" and saying that it is "as repugnant to humanity, as it is inconsistent with the Bible and destructive of liberty." He called slavery "a species of violence and tyranny" and wished the Quakers well in their "noble effort to abolish slavery."[41]

However, he then admitted to Pheasants his own sin, saying, "Would anyone believe I am the master of slaves of my own purchase! I am drawn along by the general inconvenience of living here without them." He then added, "I will not, I cannot justify it."

This, of course, opened Henry to the accusation of being insincere and hypocritical in his opposition to slavery. On the other hand, it demonstrates the power of the anti-slavery movement in Colonial America in that even slaveholders were now admitting its wickedness and sinfulness.

Thomas Jefferson

Thomas Jefferson (1743-1826) was the primary author of the Declaration of Independence and the nation's 3rd president. Although born into a slave-holding state and family,

---

[41] Patrick Henry, "Letter to Robert Pheasants," https://teachingamericanhistory.org/library/document/patrick-henry-to-robert-pleasants/.

Jefferson too came to see the evils of slavery and to call for its elimination.

During his first term in the Virginia House of Burgess, Jefferson proposed legislation to emancipate slaves in Virginia, but the motion was defeated. In a document for Virginia delegates to the Continental Congress, Jefferson called for an end to the slave trade, writing,

> The abolition of domestic slavery is the great object of desire in these colonies where it was unhappily introduced in our infant state.

In an early draft of the Declaration of Independence, Jefferson attacked the King of England and accused him of introducing slavery into the Colonies, saying,

> He has waged cruel war against human nature itself, violating its most sacred rights of life and liberty in the persons of a distant people who never offended him, captivating them and carrying them into slavery in another hemisphere.[42]

The above statement did not make it to the final draft. However, there is no question that the one that did make the final draft was a direct attack on the institution of slavery. Jefferson wrote,

---

[42] Matthew Spalding, "How to Understand Slavery and the American Founding," *The Heritage Foundation*, https://www.heritage.org/american-founders/report/how-understand-slavery-and-the-american-founding.

> We hold these truths to be self-evident, that all men are created equal, that they are endowed by their Creator with certain unalienable Rights, that among these are Life, Liberty, and the pursuit of Happiness.

They Were Considered Extremist at the Time

Dr. Martin Luther King, Jr. rightly understood this phrase to be an attack on slavery. When someone suggested to him that he was an "extremist," he replied, "Was not Thomas Jefferson an extremist? – 'We hold these truths to be self-evident, that all men are created equal.'"

Indeed, in the 18th century, when humanity was greatly divided and slavery was practiced throughout the world, the words of Jefferson were considered "extreme." When judged in the context of the times in which they lived, the Founders were, indeed, revolutionaries on the cutting edge of human society in advocating for the abolition of slavery and liberty for all mankind.

They Put Their Lives on the Line for Liberty

It is commonly taught today that America's Founders were looking out for themselves when they formed this nation. Nothing could be further from the truth. They all knew they were putting their lives at risk by signing the Declaration of Independence. They knew that King George would view their actions as an act of treason and would target them for capture or assassination.

Knowing the dangerous path onto which they were entering, in the final paragraph of the Declaration, they declared their trust in God and pledged their lives, fortunes, and sacred honor to one another. It reads,

> And for the support of this declaration, with a firm reliance on the protection of Divine Providence, we mutually pledge to each other our Lives, our Fortunes, and our sacred Honor.

After signing the document, John Hancock exhorted, "We must all hang together." Franklin, with his typical wit, is said to have quipped, "Yes, if we do not all hang together, we will surely all hang separately."

Franklin was right for they were targeted by the British for capture, persecution, and death. Of the 56 who signed the Declaration, nine died of wounds or hardships during the war. Five were captured and imprisoned, in each case, enduring brutal treatment. Several lost wives, sons, or entire families. One lost his thirteen children. Two wives were brutally treated.

All were, at one time or another, the victims of manhunts and were driven from their homes. Twelve signers had their homes completely burned. Seventeen lost everything they owned. Yet not one defected or went back on his pledged word.[43]

---

[43] Novak, 157-58.

John Adams expressed the costly sacrifice of obtaining freedom in a letter to his wife, Abigail, dated April 26, 1777. He wrote,

Posterity! You will never know, how much it cost the present Generation, to preserve your Freedom! I hope you will make a good use of it. If you do not, I shall repent in Heaven, that I ever took half the Pains to preserve it.

Chapter 5

They Grapple with Slavery In Forming a Union

> *But don't pretend that it was an easy answer—or that those who grappled with the dilemma in the 18th century were some special villains when most leaders and most people around the world saw nothing wrong with slavery.*
>
> Thomas Sowell

That the Founders came to view slavery as sinful and immoral is obvious from their own writings. However, what to do now with a massive slave population that was not prepared for freedom and whose servitude was entangled in the economy and culture of the South was another question. Sowell has written,

> Deciding that slavery was wrong was much easier than deciding what to do with millions of people from another continent, of another race, and without any historical preparation for living as free citizens in a society like that of the United States, where they were 20 percent of the population. It is clear from the private correspondence of Washington, Jefferson, and

many others that their moral rejection of slavery was unambiguous, but the practical question of what to do now had them baffled. That would remain so for more than half a century.[44]

At the Constitutional Convention in 1787, the Founders grappled with how to bring the southern states into the Union without affirming slavery. They knew that if the southern states were not included, they would align with the British or other European powers and be a constant threat to the existence of the new nation. How to include them without affirming slavery was the challenge.

In the end, concessions were made to the southern states, but as Sowell has said,

> But don't pretend that it was an easy answer—or that those who grappled with the dilemma in the 18th century were some special villains when most leaders and most people around the world saw nothing wrong with slavery.

Emotions ran high at the Convention as they grappled with the dilemma. Puritan and Awakening preachers had warned that since nations cannot be rewarded and punished in the next life, they must be in this one. They, therefore, warned of coming judgement if slavery was not ended.

---

[44] Sowell, "Twisted History," https://townhall.com/columnists/thomassowell/2003/12/17/twisted-history-n1057496

George Mason, a delegate from Virginia, expressed this same view to the Convention. He wanted slavery outlawed immediately and warned the Convention,

> Every master is born a petty tyrant. They bring the judgment of Heaven upon a country. As nations cannot be rewarded or punished in the next world, they must be in this. By an inevitable chain of causes and effects, Providence punishes national sins by national calamities.[45]

Many believe that the Civil War with its devastating loss of life and property was a fulfillment of Mason's warning of God's judgment.

Even before the Convention, in 1781, Thomas Jefferson had issued a similar warning as Morris, for it was in the context of the continuance of slavery in that South that he declared,

> God who gave us life, gave us liberty. And can the liberties of a nation be thought secure when we have removed their only firm basis, a conviction in the minds of the people that these liberties are a gift from God? That they are not to be violated but with His wrath? Indeed, I tremble for my country

---

[45] Jonathan Eliot, ed., *The Debates in the Several State Constitutions on the Adoption of the Federal Constitution as Recommended by the General Convention at Philadelphia in 1787* (Philadelphia: J.B. Lippincott Co., 1836), 458.

when I reflect that God is just and that His justice cannot sleep forever.[46]

Even with concessions to the southern states, the Founders were able to formulate a constitution that stopped the spread of slavery beyond where it had already taken root in the southern states. They also worded the Constitution so that the rights guaranteed therein could never be denied a person on the basis of race, ethnicity, or skin color. They purposely formulated the nation's fundamental legal document as a legal weapon that could be used to eventually eliminate the institution they had come to abhor.

America's 6th President Affirms the Founders

John Quincy Adams, son of John and Abigail Adams and America's 6th president, affirmed the good faith and integrity of the Founders in dealing with slavery. Commenting on the appearance of inconsistency in the founding documents that "all men are created equal" and the existence of slavery at the time, he wrote,

> No charge of insincerity or hypocrisy can be fairly laid to their charge. Never from their lips was heard one syllable of attempt to justify the institution of slavery. They universally considered it as a reproach fastened upon them by the unnatural stepmother country and saw that before the Declaration of Independence slavery, in common with every mode

---

[46] Thomas Jefferson, "Notes on the State of Virginia, Query XVIII: Manners, Thomas Jefferson/1781,"
https://teachingamericanhistory.org/library/document/notes-on-the-state-of-virginia-query-xviii-manners/

of oppression, was destined sooner or later to be banished from the earth.

The former slave and abolitionist, Frederick Douglass (1818–1895), came to this same understanding concerning the Founders. No one was more scathing in their verbal attacks on slavery and its proponents than Douglass; but after much study and investigation, he obtained a very high regard for the Founders. In a July 4th speech in 1852, he referred to the U.S. Constitution as "a glorious liberty document" and said of the Founding Fathers,

> Fellow Citizens, I am not wanting in respect for the fathers of this republic. The signers of the Declaration of Independence were brave men. They were great men too—great enough to give fame to a great age. It does not often happen to a nation to raise, at one time, such a number of truly great men.

Chapter 6

America's Colorblind Founding Documents

> *I still have a dream. It is a dream deeply rooted in the American dream.*
>
> Dr. Martin Luther King, Jr.

Because America's Founders turned against slavery, there are no classifications based on race or skin color in America's founding documents. Neither is there any mention of slaves or slavery. The language was purposeful for James Madison, the chief architect of the Constitution, said, "The Convention thought it wrong to admit in the Constitution the idea that there could be property in men."

Nothing in either the Declaration of Independence or the United States Constitution indicates that the freedoms guaranteed do not apply to every individual. Indeed, the founding generation viewed the Declaration of Independence and Constitution as anti-slavery documents and abolitionists quoted from them in their fight against slavery.

For example, in the 1852 speech mentioned above, Frederick Douglass also mentioned the Declaration of Independence and then exhorted his audience,

> The principles contained in that instrument are saving principles. Stand by those principles, be true to them on all occasions, in all places, against all foes, and at whatever cost."

Douglass obviously believed the founding documents to be an important key for ending slavery, and on another occasion, declared, "Anyone of these provisions in the hands of abolition statesmen, and backed by a right moral sentiment would put an end to slavery in America."[47]

Dr. Martin Luther King, Jr. (1929–1968) also understood this and in his stirring, *I Have a Dream* speech, he challenged America, not to dispense with her founding documents, but instead, to live up to them. Speaking from the steps of the Lincoln Memorial, he declared,

> When the architects of our Republic wrote the magnificent words of the Constitution and the Declaration of Independence, they were signing a

---

[47] David Azerrad, "What the Constitution Really Says about Race and Slavery," The Heritage Foundation, https://www.heritage.org/the-constitution/commentary/what-the-constitution-really-says-about-race-and-slavery.

promissory note to which every American was to fall heir. This note was a promise that all men, yes, Black men as well as White men, would be guaranteed the "unalienable Rights" of "Life, Liberty and the pursuit of Happiness."

Then quoting from the Declaration of Independence, he proclaimed,

I have a dream that one day this nation will rise up and live out the true meaning of its creed: "We hold these truths to be self-evident, that all men are created equal.

The Three-Fifths Clause

One of the most misunderstood sections of the Constitution is the so-called *three-fifths clause* in which only three-fifths of the slave population of southern states would be counted for representation.

This had nothing to do with assigning value based on race, as many have alleged. It was about keeping power out of the hands of the southern states.

The number of representatives from each state in Congress would be determined by the population of the state. The pro-slavery delegates from the South wanted to include slaves in the count in order increase their numbers and influence in Congress.

It was the anti-slavery delegates who pushed for the *three-fifths clause*, not to dehumanize slaves, but to penalize slave-holding states by reducing their representation in

Congress.

That the clause did not apply to all Blacks is obvious, for at the time there were at least 60,000 free Blacks in northern and southern states who counted the same as Whites when it came to determining the number of representatives to Congress. Additionally, it is important to note that there were as many as ten states where Blacks had full voting privileges.

Even here, the Founders did not use the word "slaves" or "slavery," but "other persons." Abraham Lincoln (1809–1865) described this refusal of the Founders to acknowledge slavery in the Constitution as being like a man who hides an ugly, cancerous growth until the time comes that it can be eradicated from his body.

Again, the *three-fifths clause* was not about assigning value based on race. It was a tool for keeping power out of the hands of southern states who would use such power to expand slave-holding rights to areas of the country where it was now forbidden.

An Amazing Achievement

Showing they were serious about stopping further expansion of slavery, the Founders outlawed slavery in the newly formed Northwest Territory—the future states of Ohio, Indiana, Michigan, Illinois, and Wisconsin. They worded the Constitution in such a way that the rights guaranteed therein could never be denied to anyone based on race or skin color. In formulating the founding documents, the Founders dealt slavery a mortal blow,

56

from which it would not recover.

Secularists love to insist that America was founded on racist principles. They are wrong. The historian, David Azerrad, was correct when he said, "The argument that the Constitution is racist suffers from one fatal flaw; the concept of race does not exist in the Constitution.[48]

The Founders did not invent slavery. They were born into a world where slavery already existed and was accepted all over the world. They were not perfect, and it can be argued that they conceded too much at the time. Nonetheless, they did an admirable job of formulating founding documents that would eventually eradicate slavery and make America *the land of the free and home of the brave*, with people of every race and ethnicity wanting to live here.

---

[48] Azerrad, "What the Constitution Really Says About Race and Slavery," https://www.heritage.org/the-constitution/commentary/what-the-constitution-really-says-about-race-and-slavery.

Chapter 7

Lincoln & King Build on the Foundation of the Founders

> *We will win our freedom because of the sacred heritage of our nation and the eternal will of God are embodied in our echoing demands.*
>
> Dr. Martin Luther King, Jr.

The history is clear. America's Founders are not deserving of the vicious attacks being levelled at them by radical, leftwing activists. The late Dr. Walter Williams, who happened to be Black, spoke pointedly of those activists who seek to trash America's Founders and the founding documents they produced. He wrote,

> Here's my hypothesis about people who use slavery to trash the Founders: They have contempt for our constitutional guarantees of liberty. Slavery is merely a convenient moral posturing tool they use in their attempt to reduce respect for our Constitution.[49]

---

[49] Walter Williams, "Slavery is Neither Strange nor Peculiar," *The Daily Home*, May 28, 2019,
https://www.annistonstar.com/the_daily_home/free/walter-williams-slavery-is-neither-strange-nor-peculiar-column/article_a6d802dc-815d-11e9-8947-0725f31244b3.html

At a time when slavery was accepted and practiced around the world, there was general agreement that the Founders had laid a foundation and set the nation on a course toward abolition and racial equality. The Founders expressed hope that those who would come after them would build on that foundation and move the nation forward in the goal of complete abolition.

However, they did not envision the invention of the cotton gin in 1798, which would make growing cotton a very profitable enterprise, especially when coupled with slave labor. This created an unanticipated surge of slavery in the South, delayed the expectation of the Founders, and confirmed the words of Paul the Apostle in I Timothy 6:10, *For the love of money is a root for all kinds of evil*.

Nonetheless, later advocates for abolition and racial equality, such as Abraham Lincoln and Dr. King, understood the importance of building on the foundation already laid by the Founders.

Lincoln Builds on the Foundation

Abraham Lincoln understood this. When the Republican Party was formed in 1854, its founding members promised to defeat, "those twin relics of barbarism: slavery and polygamy." In 1858, Lincoln, who became the party's first candidate for president, declared that the anti-slavery vision of the new party was the same as that of the nation's Founders. He said,

> In the way our Fathers originally left the slavery question, the institution was in the course of

59

ultimate extinction, and the public mind rested in the belief that it was in the course of ultimate extinction. All I have asked or desired is that it should be placed back again upon the bases that the Fathers of our government originally placed it upon.

Dr. King Builds on the Dream

Dr. Martin Luther King, Jr. also understood and respected the dream of America's Founders for a land of individual and religious liberty.

Writing from the Birmingham jail, he based his hope for racial equality in America on his faith in God and his faith in America as a land with a "sacred heritage." He wrote,

> We will win our freedom because **the sacred heritage of our nation** and the eternal will of God are embodied in our echoing demands.

In his iconic *I Have a Dream* speech, he clearly rooted his dream for racial equality in this original dream of America's Founders, and declared, "I have a dream. It is a dream deeply rooted in the American dream."

It was no coincidence that Dr. King delivered his *I Have a Dream* speech from the steps of the Lincoln Memorial in Washington, D.C. In his speech, he identified with both Lincoln and America's Founders in his struggle for racial equality.

It was because of the dream of America's Founders, of Lincoln, and of those standing before him, that he believed his four children would one day,

> Live in a nation where they will not be judged by the color of their skin but by the content of their character.

Standing for the American Dream

The American dream of a moral, colorblind society that guarantees individual and religious liberty for all is worth standing for. By colorblind we do not mean that we do not recognize and appreciate our unique racial and cultural backgrounds. It means that we do not use these as a basis for assigning worth and making value judgments regarding our neighbors.

This was the dream of America's Founders, Lincoln, and King and it was the dream and vision of the earliest Christians as expressed by Paul the Apostle in Galatians 3:28 where he said,

> For as many of you as were baptized into Christ have put on Christ. There is neither Jew nor Greek, there is neither slave nor free, there is neither male nor female; for you are all one in Christ Jesus.

Paul did not mean that these racial, sexual, and class distinctions no longer existed, but that the Christian did not use them to make value judgments, as did the world in which they lived. They lived by a new value system "in Christ" in which race, sex, and class were no longer the basis for judging a person's character and worth.

We don't gloss over the sins of slavery, segregation, and

discrimination in America's history, but we recognize the hand of God in the midst of the sin. Recognizing the grace of God in our past can give us hope for the future. It did so for President Lincoln, Dr. King, and thousands of others who have fought the good fight for peace, harmony, and justice in America.

If we will embrace the dream of America's Founders, Lincoln, and King, and the God they served, America could once again be a beacon of hope and freedom to all of mankind.

Epilogue

A Populist Uprising

> *All tyranny needs to gain a foothold*
> *is for people of good conscience to remain silent.*
> Thomas Jefferson

The U.S. Constitution begins with the words, "We the people." At the Constitutional Convention, the Founders saw themselves as working on behalf of the people they represented. They envisioned a nation governed, not by monarchs, oligarchs, or professional politicians, but by the people through their elected representatives and by making their voices known in all sorts of public venues.

Because they wanted a government of the people, the Founders instituted the First Amendment to the Constitution. This Amendment guarantees, not only freedom of religion, but also freedom of speech, freedom of the press, freedom to peaceably assemble, and the freedom to petition the government for a redress of grievances.

We Must Break the Silence

Thomas Jefferson said, "All tyranny needs to gain a foothold is for people of good conscience to remain silent." Where the light does not shine, darkness prevails. When "we the people" are silent, evil gains the upper hand.

It is time for "we the people" in America to break our silence. We can take back America from the socialists, secularists, and Marxists through prayer and by breaking the silence and letting our voices be heard. It is our duty as Christians and our right as Americans.

I encourage you to begin now to pray, along with thousands of others, for another Great Awakening across our land. A strong moral and Christian presence is necessary for maintaining our Constitutional freedoms, for as John Adams said,

> Our Constitution was made only for a moral and religious people. It is wholly inadequate for the government of any other."[50]

It's Time to Act

Take the truths of this book and share them everywhere. Share them with friends and your pastor. Share them with teachers, principals, and superintendents. Share them in board rooms and city council meetings. Let them know that America's Founders were on the right side of history, opposing slavery at a time it was accepted and practiced throughout the world.

Such a positive and proactive "populist uprising" of "we the people" will change America. The word "populist"

---

[50] From John Adams to Massachusetts Militia, 11 October 1798, https://founders.archives.gov/documents/Adams/99-02-02-3102

refers to common, everyday people—"we the people." **By "uprising" I simply mean that these common, everyday people are arising, praying, taking a stand, and letting their voices be heard.**

Return to the Old Paths

Each new generation likes to think that wisdom and virtue has begun with it. In so many cases, the opposite is true, as is the case in America today and was the case in Israel during the time of Jeremiah the prophet.

During a time of moral decline, social unrest, and enemies at their gates, God gave Israel the answer through Jeremiah. In Jeremiah 6:16, the prophet declared to King Josiah and all the people,

> Thus says the LORD: "Stand in the ways and see, and ask for the old paths, where the good way is, and walk in it; then you will find rest for your souls.

Just as Israel, in the time of Jeremiah, had strayed from the good way that had produced peace and prosperity, America has strayed from the way that made her the freest and most prosperous nation in history.

If we are to remain free and prosperous, we must return to those old paths—those founding principles that made America great. They are not political in nature, nor do they have anything to do with race. They are principles that will work wherever and whenever they are implemented, for they are ubiquitous and eternal in nature. They are the principles of America's Founders, of Lincoln, and of King.

About the Author

Dr. Eddie L. Hyatt is an ordained minister with 50+ years of ministerial experience as a pastor, teacher, revivalist, and professor of theology. He holds the Doctor of Ministry degree from Regent University as well as the M.Div. and M.A. (historical/theological studies) from Oral Roberts University. A prolific writer, he has authored numerous books, including *2000 Years of Charismatic Christianity*, which is used as a textbook in colleges and seminaries around the world. He has ministered in many nations through the years promoting "Spiritual Awakening and Biblical Thinking." His current passion and commission is to call America back to her founding principles of freedom and Spiritual awakening. He is doing this through his writings and through the *1726 PROJECT*, a presentation which includes visual aids using Power Point that is based on the contents of his recent book, *1726: The Year that Defined America*. Dr. Hyatt resides in Grapevine, TX with his wife, Dr. Susan Hyatt, where they are establishing the International Christian Women's Hall of Fame, Research and Ministry Center.

CONTACT INFORMATION
EMAIL: dreddiehyatt@gmail.com
WEBISITE: www.eddiehyatt.com
REGULAR MAIL: P. O. Box 3877, Grapevine, TX 76099

Selected Bibliography

Amos, Gary and Richard Gardiner. *Never Before in History: America's Inspired Birth*. Richardson, TX: Food for Thought and Ethics, 1998.

Edwards, Jonathan. *Jonathan Edwards on Revival*. Carlisle, PA: Banner of Truth Trust, 1994.

Hart, Benjamin. *Faith & Freedom: The Christian Roots of American Liberty*. Dallas: Lewis and Stanley, 1988.

Hyatt, Eddie. *1726: The Year that Defined America*. Hyatt Press: Grapevine, TX: 2019.

___. *Pilgrims and Patriots*. Grapevine, TX: Hyatt Press, 2016.

Kidd, Thomas. *God of Liberty*. New York: Basic Books, 2010.

Noll, Mark A. *A History of Christianity in the United States and Canada*. Grand Rapids: Eerdmans, 1992.

Novak, William. *On Two Wings: Humble Faith and Common Sense at the American Founding*. San Francisco: Encounter Books, 2002.

Spalding, Matthew. "How to Understand Slavery and the American Founding." *The Heritage Foundation*. https://tinyurl.com/f5kc5y8z.

Whitefield, George. *George Whitefield's Journals*. Carlisle, PA: Banner of Truth Trust, 1960.

Other Books by the Author

These and other materials are available from
Amazon and www.eddiehyatt.com.

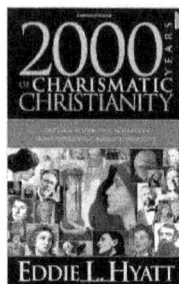

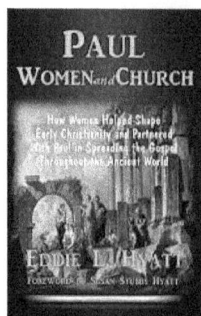

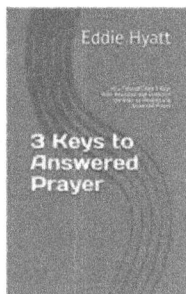

www.ingramcontent.com/pod-product-compliance
Lightning Source LLC
Chambersburg PA
CBHW071428040426
42445CB00012BA/1300